Night-Watch Man & Muse

MARK A. MURPHY

salmonpoetry

Published in 2013 by
Salmon Poetry
Cliffs of Moher, County Clare, Ireland
Website: www.salmonpoetry.com
Email: info@salmonpoetry.com

Copyright © Mark A. Murphy, 2013

ISBN 978-1-908836-57-1

All rights reserved. No part of this publication may be reproduced or transmitted in any form or by any means, electronic or mechanical, including photography, recording, or any information storage or retrieval system, without permission in writing from the publisher. The book is sold subject to the condition that it shall not, by way of trade or otherwise, be lent, resold or otherwise circulated without the publisher's prior consent in any form of binding or cover other than that in which it is published and without a similar condition, including this condition, being imposed on the subsequent purchaser.

COVER ARTWORK: *Night-Watch Man* by WILL BLACK. www.williamblack.co.uk

COVER DESIGN & TYPESETTING: *Siobhán Hutson*

Printed in Ireland by Sprint Print

Salmon Poetry gratefully acknowledges the support of The Arts Council

Acknowledgements

Acknowledgements are due to the editors of the following publications: *Albatross* (US), *Apollo's Lyre* (Canada), *The Awakening's Review* (US), *Big Pond Rumours* (Canada/Australia), *Black Mail Press* (NZ), *Both Sides Now* (US), *Canon's Mouth* (UK), *Cartier Street Review* (US), *Clean Sheets* (US), *Collective Exile* (US), *deaddrunkdublin* (Ireland), *The Delinquent* (UK), *Epiphany Magazine* (US), *Extracts* (US), *Fib Review* (US), *The Furnace Review* (US), *Glint Literary Journal* (US), The Invisible Fire Journal (US), *Iota* (UK), *Iodine Poetry Journal* (US), *The Journal* (UK), *Litspeak* (Germany), *Metazen* (US), *Munyori Literary Journal* (India), *New England Review* (Australia), *The New Verse News* (UK), *The New Writer* (UK), *Nightshift Anthology* (Five Leaves Publications) (UK), *Nthposition* (UK), *Ottowa Arts Review* (Canada), *The Outlaw Poetry Network* (France), *Paris Atlantic Journal* (France), *Peace and Freedom Press* (UK), *Pennine Ink Magazine* (UK), *The Poetry Kit Magazine* (UK), *Poetry Monthly* (UK), *Poetry New Zealand* (NZ), *Poetry Salzburg Review* (Austria), *Poetry Scotland* (UK), *Poets Against War* (US), *Puerto Del Sol* (US), *Quarterly Literature Review* (Singapore), *The Reading Life* (Philippines), *Red Ochre LiT* (US), *Red River Review* (US), *Samsara* (US), *Snakeskin* (UK), *SNReview* (US), *The Stinging Fly* (Ireland), *Stride Magazine* (UK), *SubtleTea* (UK), *Tadeeb International* (UK), *The Tampa Review* (US), *Transition Magazine* (Canada), *Valley Micro Press* (NZ), *Wordgathering* (US), *Words-Myth* (US), *WOW! Magazine* (UK).

The poem 'Manageable Space' is re-written from the original, which first appeared in my chapbook, *Tin Cat Alley* (Spout Publications, 1996).

Many thanks to Jessie and Siobhán at Salmon Poetry and to artist, Will Black, for the front cover painting.

*"Each contact with a human being is so rare,
so precious, one should preserve it."*
— Anaïs Nin

For those whom I have known and loved.

Contents

Taking Shade With Buddha	13
Affinity	14
Stonewalling	15
The Roman Laurel	16
Coniston Water	17
Manageable Space	18
Convergence	20
On Chasing Pigeons	21
The Struggle	22
Echo Forever	23
Killing the Summer	24
Song of the Grunion	25
Beach Note	26
Devotion	27
bitter sweet sonata	28
Outlaws	29
Exotic Dance	30
The Sleeping Father	31
Britain	32
Mermaid	35
Humanity	36
The Liverpool Tate	37
Girl With A Pearl Earring	38
Looking Out, Looking In	39
Rhosilli Beach	40
River Meeting	41
For Him, For Her	43
Night-Watch Man & Muse	44

Anthem In Eden	45
Allotment	46
Snowbound	47
Contrition	49
Anniversary	50
Night Photographer	51
The Kindness	52
Mr Mojo Risin'	53
Ullswater	54
In Praise Of Jikan, the Monk	55
Mirror, Mirror	56
Leave-taking	58
Death In The Sick Room	59
Saint-in-the-box	60
on exile	62
The Last Summer	63
Acantha	65
Season's End	66
Last Word	67
An Agnostic's Prayer	71
Minotaur's Woe	72
Canal Poem	73
Lost Souls	74
Solace	75
River Of Blood	76
Farewell, Leon Livovich	77
For A Fistful Of Earth	78
Calypso	79

Swamp Meeting	80
Fall From Grace	81
Ageing Sisyphus	82
Autumn Leaving	83
Mica	84
Autumn Rises	85
The Unanswered Question	86
Transformation	87
In A Rage With Allen Ginsberg	88
The Last Stand Of Salvadore Allende	89
Lonely Fighter	90
William S. Burroughs Dead	91
Seems So Long Ago	93
Requiem For A Kiss	94
Versts	95
Tonight	96
In His Time Of Dying	97
An Ending	98
Willow Lane	99
Nie przejmuj się	100
Diogenes Checkmates	101
The Zoo	102
Memorial	103
Why I Am Not A Sculptor	104

Taking Shade with Buddha

Of all the dense vegetation in this wild country
I have come to take shade with Buddha
(though he is equally at ease in sun or shadow)
under the bent branches of the Bodhi tree.

Frankly, it is not the best spot to make camp,
break the night's fast,
or break the habits of a life-time
but Buddha seems at home, like a man who has lived

irreverent aeons alone — he makes a welcome as only he can —
confident of my comings and goings, naked
as one new born, sure that living is its own answer,
he offers figs for my hunger.

Slowly then, Buddha savours the morning air
as though it were sustenance enough
while the first light bakes the land
and each man and beast in the field is busy with the crop.

Already, I am in at the deep-end with my questions:
what if the knowledge of trees is no knowledge at all —
and if the trees should support the sky no more,
and the deliberate hush in the night really is the end, then what?

But Buddha is having none of it. And indeed, why should he trouble,
being at one, as he is, with forest, sky and the hallowed ground.
And by and by a talkative brook bothers the shadows
and Buddha is smiling — pleased at the sound of water on stone.

For an instant, he is like a child who has found his mother's hand
in some crowded place and then a moment later
he is old all over again like a being who has lived many lives.
Buddha breathes deeply. He breathes in the universe.

Affinity

We are the public statues, stirring, stirring
    in the town squares at night.
We are private beings, moving, moving
    through this public space.

We are strangers in the head, clutching, clutching
    at our ribboned hats.
We are Ithaka's wings, moving, moving
    in the scattered breeze.

We are the Bronte sisters, dreaming, dreaming
    of dying, always dying.
We are Anne, Emily and Charlotte, moving, moving
    through the graveyard of our father's ministry.

We are the bronchial children, playing, playing
    in the grounds of the Parsonage.
We are the breathing ghosts, moving, moving,
    breathing and moving in the dark.

We are the human creature, crying, crying,
    treading the boards thin.
We are Balzac's cloak, moving, moving
    unceasingly in the night wind.

Stonewalling

There are words, sometimes. We cannot utter
them. Safer. Better then, we do not talk
of hearts and courses,

facing this or facing that. We know
our present business here
is to laugh.

Only, when I see the gaps, drawing me back
from distance to distance,
such simple acts:

the placing of things, for instance, that go
unnoticed. Stone upon stone.
Prayer upon prayer.

Not walling in, not walling out, just being;
I wonder at our private hurts,
divergent paths.

There are stones, sometimes. We cannot place
them. Safer. Better then, we do not talk
of hearts and courses,

facing this or facing that. Our wall
will find its own course
in time,

settle into earth, steadfast and patient,
this rock will forever echo
our passing.

The Roman Laurel
for Nicholas Christopher

Could it be the eye of man is heavenly in its nature
gazing up at the stars, as it does, to capture
something more than the sum total of its parts?

Could it be the eye of man is more lost than found
among the myriad crowds in their mourning-bands
than all the stars spiralling in the outward bounds?

How then should we look at the uttermost galaxy
if we do not see in it the remarkable choreography
of light that affects our own worldly destiny?

The eye which gazes into the glittering heavens
sees beyond the dreams of the ordinary man,
sees in the beam its own nature, its own origins.

Coniston Water

Look out across the lake.
Not to the far shore;
roads and walls that make

the manageable fragments of hills
have little to do
with what's reflected in the shrill

water about these stones.
Reach out beyond
the conifer plantations,

sail-boats and unexpected rain;
the human presence here
is large, beyond imagining.

Manageable Space

Anyone acquainted with
the ideas of Herr Freud
will be glad to learn

as I did,
that we are not alone
in our anxieties;

even the good
professor suffered
bouts of agoraphobia,

which is no laughing matter,
since the response
is one of terror.

Asked what it was
that caused the fear,
he might have said

it was his childhood,
an early memory of steam
trains, the action

of the pistons, or
that the rattling
of the carriage mimicked

death. Imagine then,
a lake or reservoir –
nothing too disturbing.

You are standing
at the water's edge,
you see yourself

from a great distance.
What do you see
but a human dot?

You need to get away
from the water, the expanse
is too much, too blue.

You need to get back
to the world
of enclosure, the world

of manageable space.
Now imagine Sigmund's train.
On such journeys

the mind is lost.
The reasonable world is lost
to the opening out

of an unfamiliar landscape,
hills and mountains,
estuaries and flood plains,

where the desire to get free
is contradicted
by the desire to hide.

At last, you can put
yourself in the shoes
of the good professor.

Convergence

How much of this is private, how much
beyond the telling, this moment stuffed
among moments, hidden in the knickers drawer
between the suspender belts, stockings
and out-of-date contraceptives:

you, who would never be photographed,
looking deep into the lens, past the spells
of sun and salt water, arms stretched to avoid
distortion, but the image still distorted,
watcher and watched, naked and remote?

On Chasing Pigeons

It is tiring just watching him chase, this way and that
undeterred by repeated failure to capture even a single bird.
What nerve, what gusto the little boy has,

much to the exasperation of his mother, who gestures
for the boy to stop clowning. Boys will always play though
and her efforts to censure his behaviour only gives rise

to renewed devotion: *Again! Again! Again!* He chants
while the birds flap above him, always out of reach
always one step ahead. Oh we know, chasing pigeons

is best left to cats, and a boy of five will never be a match
for an old town pigeon, but for today, at least,
today he has no intention of abandoning his pursuit.

The Struggle
for Suheir Hammad

Sister of mine! Dream with me under the stars
where the immense ceiling of night
covers the land and all our fears.

We are the children of the struggle,
we are the beautiful and proud ones –
we will not be silenced by violence.

All this time, we stare loss in the face
and our hearts are strengthened once more
by the courage of the landless dead.

You enemies of the people – you know
who you are – in whose name do you fight?
We will not forgive you at the end of days.

Where there was already suffering and adversity,
you have made deserts with your war machines.
Soon you too will lie buried in the ground.

And in time even this land will be free.
And the young will frown with indignation.
And they will ask, 'what was it all for?'

Echo Forever

It is not with the ease of everyday lovers
we meet on the hills of this island,
coming to the table as we do –
with our hearts in a state of mortal dislocation.

When we say, 'we do not want any more,'
it is only because the iron foot of disbelief
would stomp down joy and beauty
in the landscape of our current imaginings.

Oh no, not for us the easy bread
of first communion; we stare into the deep hole
of what went before and dream our simple plans
of a life less familiar, where the schemes

of care are given a chance to thrive
in the telling of some uncomplicated tale.
It is the armour of centuries
we disassemble every time we meet:

this is what it is to lift the cup one more time.

Killing the Summer

It is no use turning it over — except we can do little else —
caught in the grief
of our own remembering, reasoning, remorse.

This is what it is to be alive —
knowing each time we close our eyes

could be the last.
Still, it is almost unbelievable, allowing as we do:

'nothing human is alien'
that death —
untimely and uncalled for death

should come late in the afternoon
and root destruction in the brain.

Sure. It is not quite right how the kettle on the hob
outlasts the man who wrought it

or the man who supped at its spout,
not quite right how the world hums
as tragedy smacks the child in the face

declaiming those favourite words, 'you've lost again,'
and consciousness

slips from the young man's mind,
and the sick men in the abattoir skin the cattle alive.

Song of the Grunion
for Jacob Bronowski

It is time to leave these glassy shores
to those who are not yet born

and the eyes of men;
one day soon the moon will sing

her song of ascent
to the retiring waves

and we will name that song
Grunion Spring.

Beach Note

I am watching you on the beach
stepping out over the dunes with ease.

I look at your body like a man
who never saw a woman naked before.

I want to rush towards you urgently
entering you for the first time

with words only a madman would utter:
I feel elemental, like Odysseus

strapped to the mast. I want to take you
wildly, without a care, out into the storm.

Devotion

If I could win you with words
I would write, "Come and lie naked with me.
Oh, come and lie naked with me."

And you would give yourself
without hesitation in the lacerated city
of my yearly ruined dreams.

Alas, we do not live by the rules
of happy circumstance. The real story,
sad though it is, unfolds like this:

if I told you in the encroaching darkness
how much the night derides me,
you would only turn your back

and keep the moonlight for yourself.
If I told you that I held my hand
in the flame for you, I know

you would not believe me.
If I told you that I cut myself
in the dark cellars of self-knowing

for all the saints and martyrs
but most of all, for you,
I know you would only shrink back

and think me mad. If I told you
that I had stolen these seconds
from the silence that lies between us

to tell you, you are more beautiful
today than I ever imagined,
you would only recoil and say,

"You cannot win me with words."

bitter sweet sonata

i ask you to undress   you slip out of your clothes
and stalk me across the calico sheets of the unmade bed
i see your body and i want to take you into the wild
expanse of sea and space   oh let me come into your arms

let me come into your woman's place   where the sea spray
salts my lips and tongue   Lauren   this is our time
to try   sure in the knowledge that we drift endlessly
into an ocean of disasters   curious girl   seeker of truth

i love the sure way you look up at me when you kneel
so many leagues below me   taking me into your mouth
when you kiss me   i see a torrent in your eyes
you well up   overwhelming me with pure   unbridled joy

Outlaws
(for L.J.F)

When we meet like this in secret
offering up our bodies to one another,
I can't help wondering what other lives
you're involved with. Our ritual

loving leaves nothing ahead, only recall;
the exchange of blood stains
the white sheets of my conscience,
which has grown fragile over the weeks

of knowing one so forward with her body.
When I take your sex in my mouth
I'm left with the residue of bitter thoughts.
If it is so much torture to feel love –

why do we ever stray from the path?
No one reason being good enough
to stay, we make the relevant excuses;
tonight will be the last time we do this.

Exotic Dance

Night after night she gave refuge to the loneliness
of which I am made, day and then night again
she danced in the loneliest bars and in her body

I saw the dreams of a thousand girls revolving,
and in her eyes I saw a thousand yearnings, and each time
she turned, it was as if she turned just for me.

She was naked and divine, my Olympia of the ballet,
and when she moved in the half dark, the tricks of light
on her belly and her thighs made all the flesh tremble

and come alive, and I didn't care if she only remembered
my name to forget the past, I knew it wasn't for me
but when she came to me and took my hand, I loved her,

and if I had known each instance of her sexual life
intimately, I would have loved her all the same,
and if she had told me, every man who took her

took her more viciously with every coming
I would have loved her more again,
and if she had told me she had worked her body

to feed the kids, I would have given my heart to her
as surely as I would give my heart to my own mother,
and if she had told me of the violence in some men's eyes

I would have held her until the morning sky had filled
the room with light, and if she had told me she loved me
I would have been the happiest man alive.

The Sleeping Father

My father is asleep with a book over his face.
His brow is all perspiration. Beads of sweat
    roll down his chest.
    His breathing

is heavy and staggered in the dusty August heat.
I think it must be the warmest day of the summer
    so far. I watch him closely,
    taking great care

not to wake him. The gramophone spindle is loaded
with 78's performing a hushed balancing act, poised
    on the brink of something
    momentous.

A daddy-long-legs whirrs at the ceiling by the paper
lampshade. Today is a good day to be alive.
    It is a good day to be
    seven years old.

A sudden light penetrates the curtains, catching
the buckle of his wrist watch. His arms are brown
    and thick from working
    in the sun.

His shoulders are red and peeling like pomegranate.
It is an easy picture to summon. The memory
    of it is larger
    than life.

My attention wanders to some mad scheme or daydream.
I chase down the hallway in search of tin soldiers.
    I fight the battle to end
    all battles.

The house is quiet. No voices. No traffic on the road.
Just soundless heat. And my father fast asleep
    in his favourite chair,
    out like a light.

Britain

Britain my father loved W.H. Auden and all his poetics.
    I loved them both and all their after-dinner conversation
    though neither had the answers I was looking for.
Britain when I was 15 I read The Communist Manifesto.
    I fought alongside the miners – those history makers,
    those heroes of the class struggle – I thought
    we could change the world.
Britain it's 20 years since I joined the disaffected.
I never played the stock-markets.
I never climbed the social ladder or doffed the cap.
I never believed in the sanctity of the family or marriage
    or went to church on Sundays.
Britain I never learned how to kill another human being.
Britain I would've converted to Buddhism but couldn't grasp
    their need for prayer.
Britain I'm strung out with thoughts of smouldering bodies.
I'm wired with thoughts of unexploded cluster bombs
    and flattened cities.
Britain when does a bomblet cease to be a bomblet?
What is the evil scourge of terrorism?
Who will write the history of the world?
Britain I'm afraid to sleep in case I dream my dream
    of the dead.
So many millions.
So many millions of delicate humans.
So many millions, gone forever.
Britain I'm on the side of the living.
I'm larger than you think.
I contain multitudes.
All there is of love I contain it.
All there is of loss I contain it.
Britain where does the history of infamy begin –
    Ireland…North America…India?
Britain I'm the redeemer of the oppressed.

I never meant to do you harm.
I'm dying all over again.
I'm history repeating itself.
I'm the children of the Gael burning at Drogheda.
I'm the Indian nations dying of smallpox.
I'm the walking dead in the lanes of Skibbereen
I'm the ghost people of Tasmania.
I'm James Conolly, my body all holes.
I'm the city of Dresden burning by starlight.

Britain did you civilize the Mau Mau? Those damn Kikuyu
    always were trouble.
Do you still follow your humanitarian impulses?
When will you eradicate the propaganda of the left?
Britain I'm not joking.
You must defend the free world from state terror.
Britain there's no need for excuses.
There's no insignificant enemy.
You'll rewrite international law when the time comes.
Those rogue states must be dealt with.
They are like academics, with their cock-eyed view of reality.
Past atrocities can remain safely forgotten, like summer fêtes.
What everybody says must be true.
Ah, those halcyon days.
Ah, those salad days.
Ah, those heady days of empire.
Britain you do not lead the new imperial order.
You are only the junior partner.
But you must keep your eye on the ball.
Britain it's a thankless task, being faithful to the bitter end –
    O cover ups! assassinations! dirty wars!
It's time to enlist.
It's time to dole out fig leaves for the dead.
Fig leaves for the tortured.
Fig leaves for the displaced.
Fig leaves for the dispossessed.
Fig leaves for the disenfranchised.

Fig leaves for the poor.
Fig leaves for the unholy.
Fig leaves for Kosovo.
Fig leaves for Iraq.
Britain taking afternoon tea won't change history.
It won't sweeten the pill.
It won't strengthen your hand.
It won't save your skin.
Britain the future is a long time.
And the wearing of cricket whites won't impede the truth.
And the donning of tennis whites won't delay the verdict.
And being British won't excuse you from court.
And brass bands playing in park pavilions on a Sunday afternoon
    won't bring back the dead.
Britain we can be sure of this.

Mermaid

She came out of the southern ocean
steeped in mystery. Reckless as sunlight
in the winter surf, bold as morning breaking
over sand and dunes and the treeless downs.

And when the first men spied her naked
on the beech, they cried as children.
And when the women first saw her in the lanes and ginnels
of the old village, they bolted their doors

as if an ill wind were blowing. No one knew why she came
that December morning after a lifetime of centuries
alone. No one cared. But our lady of the deep
had awoken from her dreams in the bleak mid-winter

and came ashore innocent as day breaking
over the sleepy community. And no one could turn back time.
How many men had dreamt of such a creature
emerging as she did with her raven hair

tossed about her loving breasts? Of course,
it would not be long now before the doors opened
and the warmth of firelight would warm her through.
And so it began. The good men of the village

gave her refuge, but it was not long before asylum turned
to torment. Days and nights passed.
After the men had taken what they wanted
as though the taking was their given right,

they cast her out onto the cobbled walkway
like bundled flesh not fit for dogs, and when the women saw
what the men-folk had done, they rushed to condemn
our lady as a 'wanton' and 'fallen' woman.

In that time of miracles, the villagers gathered
to cast their stones at the sad figure of a mermaid drowning
in the abounding air. Her cries could not be heard
above the crashing waves. No one and nothing could save her.

Humanity

Three cheers for all those who would kiss and make up!
Three cheers for Captain Ahab's leg!
Three cheers for poetry that never gets a look in!
Three cheers for the blind hermit's barometer!
Three cheers for John Merryck!
Three cheers for life's little obstacles!
Three cheers for our ladies of the pantihose!
Three cheers for utter nonsense!
Three cheers for the telephonist's dilemma!
Three cheers for virtue!
Three cheers for 'loophole theory'!
Three cheers for the void, in whose name we take to the drink!
Three cheers for utter drunkenness!
Three cheers for the glorious martyrdom!
Three cheers for the poet's daughter in whose honour I close
    my eyes, etc, etc.!
Three cheers for the pharmacist's white coat!
Three cheers for all those who do not need three cheers!
Three cheers for all those who do!
Three cheers for the sake of having three cheers!
Three cheers most of all for you!

The Liverpool Tate

It's important to state the obvious, and audibly if you can, for the benefit of anyone in earshot. You mustn't be afraid to speak non- sense. You could say, for example, these artefacts of texture and light are keys.

The fat ungainly maiden being rescued from a puny dragon.

The stork foiling the fox.

The nuclear wife and daughter struggling to dress dad.

The family group being a family group, being a family group, being...

But nothing's clear, certainly not as a clear as it seems, not even the view of the Mersey through the mottled glass, the muted shrieks of white rags in the estuary, scraps of light.

I wonder where all this scrutiny will lead, and what the two slim and lovely students will make of Paula Rego's grotesque ballerinas.

Girl with a Pearl Earring *

I have undressed you once again,
though I have no special prerogative to do so.

I am neither the artist, or your man,
yet my eyes insist on robbing what's left of your innocence.

Your mouth parts as you look from your repose
as though you are about to say something

and I am captivated by the perfection of your mouth
as though it were the only mouth in all creation.

When I look in your eyes,
I am broken by the miracle of conception.

Neither geography or the centuries can separate us,
neither religion or social standing can keep us apart.

We are alone together, caught up in this moment
like no other two beings on earth.

I feel your breath on my neck, I feel the warmth of your thighs
and I am as far beyond sin as is possible.

What doubts come to us now are older
than any plots of our making.

What dreams are discarded in favour of a sober life,
flare up and are lost in an instant.

An hour moves the world off its axis –
once there was a past and then there is nothing.

Griet, I have undressed you once again. What for?
For art's sake, always for art's sake.

* *Painted 1665 – 1666 by Jan Vermeer*

Looking Out, Looking In

It is not the sky opening that wakes you,
the sound of morning against canvass,
voices, vehicles, children playing,
not the sound of sea or the feel
of dew underfoot, but the longing to share

this beach, this path above the cliffs,
the spectacle of beetle pursuing snail
over yellow gorse, the minute
reminding us of what we are; vulnerable,
mortal, at odds with ourselves, and yet

today our hearts are lighter. After all,
the sea is not so big that it cannot be
sailed, and love not so fraught
that it cannot be lived. Despite
the warp and weft of ordinary grief,

the proliferation of rock-falls and rock-pools,
dead starfish and tiny crabs going
about their crabby business, some dying,
some living, all paths lead me back to you;
this is home and this is where the heart is.

Rhosilli Beach

It is not the wreckage that invites
me to this spot, ocean, sand dunes,
outcrops of rock, but your hand

held aloft, childlike in the wind.
Mysteries, worlds and years apart;
as sun and tide rescind, and hills

that mark the skyline, echo
the shadows of sea-birds;
our feet will tread the wet sand

where no two feet have trod,
our imprints here, fleeting
but for love.

River Meeting

Life is simple for the coracle man,
his face is old and unassuming.
It is the kind of face that knows acceptance.
He belongs to a different time.

A time when the river could breathe more easily,
a time before the city's madness
and shared boredom, a time
before the river cruise and tourist trap.

Clear and steady as the iron
that spans the space between the banks,
he watches the changing seasons
and fashions his craft. The last of his kind.

He is not much given to conversation,
but when he chooses, he talks about the river
like another man might talk
about a wife or lover;

her changing moods, her sudden swells,
the dazzle of sunlight at dawn and dusk,
the suck of the moon on inland tides,
the firelight of far-off stars.

He knows all about the ripples of breathing fish,
only moments away from the surface,
the dip and skim of the cormorant's beak,
the floods and loops of geological time.

She is ice in the night, polished obsidian
that captures the shadows
of night geese and alighting swans,
the somnambulist's dream of morning.

It is June. The river is calm.
It flows quietly now
along the Seven Valley Gorge
down through Coalbrookdale,

under the Ironbridge and calmly on
past the coracle man's house.
If you find him there, stretching hide
and bending willow, ask after him a while.

Doubtless, he will tell you there is nothing to say
of his life away from the river.
No past to speak of. No children or wife.
Only that he makes coracles. It is what he has always done.

For Him, For Her

I will name a star in the remote reaches of the Lost Galaxy
for my father who sits alone in his study playing chess
and celestial dice, whilst perfecting his old mystic's hunch.

But this will be as nothing, when compared to my planet-sized
generosity towards my children who are not yet born.
For them, I will buy ten acres of lunar dust on the light side of the moon.

And for my children's children, I will buy the rocky plains of Venus,
and when I am done with buying planets, I will buy race horses
and golden hollow heart necklaces for the ladies of solitude.

And for the memory of dead lovers, I will buy ice-bergs and deserts,
unfathomable gifts for the unravelling of time, where the phantasms
in the brain wreak havoc over the hearts and minds of the living man.

And for my only godchild, I will buy a dolly and for his mother,
I will buy a long lost title of a long dead royal, and for the brave man
and the fool, there will be golden tokens placed on their eyes
> when they sleep.

For the newly weds down the lane, I will buy vintage champagne,
and for the maids in the grand hotel, they shall have roses in their bowers
and bathe in the milk of does before the hotel manager and the Pope.

And last of all – and just for you – I will ignore the shrieks in the Sultan's
harems, and the horn that would sound the end of time and I will buy
the Rubaiyate of Omar Khayyam, and we will learn to live ungodly lives.

Night-Watch Man & Muse

I watch over the town like a lost angel
just beginning to grasp the significance of my task.
Where ever you are asleep, I hear the sounds
of sleep-walkers, sleep-talkers and sleep-junkies – too tired
to mutter more than the odd syllable about growing old,
reciting the names of ex-lovers and sweet-hearts
as though their litanies would bring back
the lost, the wounded, the deceased
for that one last conversation that would change everything.
They talk the honest talk of the subconscious mind
(allowing as we do for the affairs of translation)
and we must congratulate them on their night babble.
Never again will Jill tell Jack the truth – only in dreams.
And what of the truth, undependable as it is, changeable
as always by the way the light catches valleys and peaks.
My task is simply to watch and listen whilst
the last of the party goers take themselves home
and the very last stragglers, who have lost their sense
of what is right and wrong, think their way
into the bedrooms of the handsome and the beautiful.
I do not seek to order the night, I hear the lonely
the sick, the maligned, the disparate voices
of a town groaning under the weight of its own contradictions
and offer comfort in the long hours when no other voice
but the stranger's voice on the phone will do.

Anthem In Eden

It is not without reason the sky opens
to us as we open to it. We have passed
through so many nights of disbelieving,
it hardly seems plausible to start over.

Where will it take us? No one knows.
But when the stars draw closer
in their millions to greet the living
eye, anything becomes possible.

When the doubts of centuries burden
us with their prayers we will assume
for a day the knowledge all creation knows –
what has a beginning must also end.

But when I watch you cross the room,
the smallest gestures of your hips
command all of my attention, as though
to say, forget what we cannot know

what we cannot change, love is upon us.

Allotment

    Look out from this island, now,
see the spaces where we live,
    tread down bracken and bramble,
move aside the broken twig.

    Stare down from this hill top, stuffed
between city and suburb, stadium
    and village green, frost on the stem
of a leaf and the child's eye view.

    Down there in the valley bottom –
you will see your allotted ground,
    thickets of terraces gathered into streets,
huddled in defiance of death.

    Strange, this space caught between
places, among the chicken wire and dens,
    scarecrows and glass-house neglect;
see what you've missed; prints in the snow

    fixed amid the dereliction of occasion,
frozen in the snowy earth, reflecting
    the passage of moments from one time
to the next, one season to another.

Snowbound

Two boys are playing in the snow. They are waiting
for the sky to turn. When it gets dark, they will make
their way to the woods for firewood. Inside the house
their mother rummages through the pantry, considering

the value of things. She draws the fire with a sheet
of newspaper, melts lard and candle wax over the last
fragments of coal in the Ray burn, burns margarine tubs,
off cuts of carpet, cardboard, anything that will flame.

She watches them with care, her breath clearly visible
against the delicate latticing of ice on the frozen glass,
frowning now and again when a missile drops too close
to the dining room window. The snow falls heavily

and evenly. 'Saw only the fallen trees,' she advises,
feeding the fire with an old shoe, 'the new growth
just doesn't take.' Damp winter clothes and bed linen
hang over the angled stove-pipe and copper fire-guard.

In the woods now, past signs marked 'Private' and 'Keep Out',
our little woodcutters busy themselves with chopping,
sawing and collecting. What can't be taken this trip
will save for next time, stored in pyramids in the secret

interiors of holly bushes. Loading their makeshift carts,
they turn and make for home to the pebble-dashed semi
on Stoney Lane. Knee deep through drifts they trudge
and laugh over the last of the milkman's fields and back

onto the estate with its intimate smells of coke, coal
and wood smoke, bypassing Long Lane, they arrive
breathless and shaking. The soot from burning rubbish
falls to the ground, comes to rest in the fresh snow.

As grown men, we sit in the cold of some other place drinking cheap beer from tins, going over those past events, wondering what's changed, our lives no less fraternal than then, only the question still lingers.

Why bother to remember? And then it strikes me, the way memory can sometimes overwhelm you. Perhaps the sun was especially bright this morning, perhaps it was the image of the soot speckled snow.

Contrition

Hold me till morning comes,
catch my conceit in all its forms.

Take away all the forfeits
assembling in the night

that would capture the beating heart.
If we must linger in this dark,

as lovers sometimes might,
let our guide be love not hate.

Let stars go out if it be there fate,
we will soon be home, safe.

Anniversary

As the night comes and goes without trace,
so the years come and go without any hint
of us ever having been and we pass
on the stairs as if these ten years of our passing

meant nothing. Perhaps it was impossible
for me to tell you stories to make your dreams.
Now my ordinary sober world wishes to catch
a knowing glance, a last smile of approval.

I catch your scent as you gather your self up
to leave this place for some other shore.
Soon only memory will account
for your presence in these dim rooms.

I imagine you on the night ferry to Dublin:
your man cradles your head in his arms.
The sea is calm, your children sleep beside you,
time hardly matters outside this family group.

What's past and gone into myth matters
less and less. We hardly understand.
We who are left behind, made up
as we are of our own doubts and longings

look after you with all the sadness of old age
and though we are not yet old ourselves,
we feel the future beckoning like some new
decade which does not yet belong to us.

Night Photographer

I possess you in photographs. I possess you…

> night after night your body opens
> to my eye and I am silent beside you
> like a man who only knows pain
> lost in sad reflection and prayer.

It was no accident that I came to take you in this way.
I made no secret of my ragged heart or the tenderness
that ran in my veins for you like exhausted sonnets.
I needed your embrace like the kiss of a child.

I have mapped the lines and freckles in your face
and each tiny scar and mole that adorn your body
as if they were jewels put there just for my discovery.
I felt like Columbus bringing gold to the King of Spain,

but the more you said you loved him, the more I looked
to see if there was something I had missed, some omen,
or some clue, any clue to undo the spell you were under.
The more you said you loved him, the more I wanted you.

> Then, I see you as a little girl
> and I am drawn into you
> even more surely than before.
> I wish you were my little girl,

I wish I could hold your hand and guide you home
every time you felt lost or alone or hurt. I wish I could
ward off all the little tragedies that go to make up a life,
but I am as helpless before your past as any man

who tried to love you. You made a gift of your body.
And I am a man in possession of little else; prepared
for a battle, a war, anything. No matter, that you vanished
before the first roll of the dice. You are free now.

My wild eyed girl. My wide eyed girl.

The Kindness

You are naked again, this time
bending over the bed, tending to me
as though I were your only lover.

You kiss me gently, your moist lips parting
upon touching, first my forehead,
both my eyelids, and then my mouth

as if you were making love to me
slowly, surely with just your mouth –
for the first time, all over again.

Mr Mojo Risin'

Of all the poets in this city of the dead
I make my way to your grave.
I do not come for words, tears, rancour.

Dear friend, I came to tell you
if there is any comfort to be had,
anything at all, it is this…

out here on the edge of darkness
there is no death,

only freedom — all consuming freedom.
But then I guess you knew that.

Now a group of Spanish girls are laying flowers.

They are saying, 'cruel satyr
with your tongue on fire… why did you die?'

Satyr says nothing at all.

Ullswater

It is not with any apology we walk
the silt and pebble of this shoreline –
through time and space we ache

to crack the spell our other selves
have made. Although we are not new
there is reason enough to misbehave.

Because there is no other place
where branch and twig mend
and past and present interlace

we spend the day tranquil as rain
not yet fallen. This is the first leaf
of the season, the first primrose

of spring, the first kiss to take
form – whispered in the morning
with delicate breath. See.

There is no one else here besides us.
We make the lake our own –
the whole thing is possible. At once

the cirrus sky asserts its living
breath and we breathe certain
in the knowledge of our simple

passing; Gowbarrow behind,
Birk Fell before, and the journey
to and from only just begun.

In Praise of Jikan, the Monk
for Leonard Cohen

I give you those drunken nights on Trinity Street
and the young girls in the degenerate air
although you do not wish for them.

You have your own drunken nights
among the lovelorn
and forlorn young women in their thigh-high boots.

Certainly, I am not here to lay claim
to anything beyond the dull circumstance
of my own downfall.

There are no secrets I can tell you.
I damaged every woman I ever loved.
I risked it all in my pursuit of innocence.

I used to think I could shoulder
another's pain as if it were my own,
I thought I could rescue the fallen and the lame –

when I could not even prevent my own disgrace,
or find a justification
for my wayward sensibilities.

I give you my girlfriend's telephone number,
safe in the knowledge
that I can no longer satisfy her.

If I had only one minute left to live,
I would give it up, listening to you, singing:
where do all these highways go, now that we are free…

Mirror, Mirror

I take it as the final insult, the final hurt
in a life made up of little else.
I was an ideal woman once, the kind
of woman you only dreamed existed,
and so skinny in fact, so unlike a woman
that men would applaud me on my boyish figure.
I was loved by men for my flat chest,
my pretty little ass, my sweet little ass –
not a dimple in sight. I was the purest girl
at the disco, a virgin until I was 26.
God, how I was loved by men.

Now, even starlight does nothing
for my complexion. I have nothing
to show but my mother's bitter frown,
a bitter frown with which I view the world.
My breasts have become zealous balloons.
My thighs are ruined.
I look in the mirror, see
my whole tawdry past spread-eagled,
other faces, other bodies, lives assembling
like gilt at the mirror's edge.

Mirror, mirror, on the wall, oldest
and wisest of all my mirrors:
my confidant, my window on the confessional,
my window to other mirrors...
won't you tell me what I cannot tell myself:
that it didn't matter as long
as they loved me for my lily-white thighs?
Won't you tell me
that I am still beautiful –
a beautiful coat hanger woman?

2

Mirrors in the kitchen.
Mirrors in the bathroom.
Mirrors in the bedroom.
Even the juxtapositioning of mirrors.
Ceiling mirrors.
Wall mirrors.
Door mirrors.
Nothing but mirrors.

This is not living.
This is mirror hell.

Leave-taking

I take my hand away from your breast.
I take it away. I take it away.
I watch your back – it is long and perfect.
It moves away. It moves away.

We would not kiss and yet the ache
remains as if the two could never part.
There are no rhymes possible, no reasons
adequate to denote an ending

and yet the end is no more demanding
than what is plainly felt in the clear night.
To be alone and never to have loved
each other; sure, this would be sin enough

before the gods of heaven and earth.
But whatever outcomes will be made
by errant dreamers, the parting gift will bring
its own joy and unlock the far off stars.

Death in the Sickroom

Who knows more than children
that death leaves its own disagreeable malady
in the minds of the living siblings?

All the wringing of hands in the sickroom,
the necessary prayer, the clasping
of hands held in resignation and despair,

each man and woman – ultimately alone
in the houses of their upbringings,
ineluctably aware of their own demise.

They talk in careful whispers, even now,
behind the shuttered windows,
where the human family gathers in unity

of purpose, whilst the bespectacled doctor
and bearded passer-by are never far
enough away from the apprehension

of their own untimely passing;
this is how it is with the pain of separation,
when we look into the green rooms

of loss with their polished wooden floors
where we turn our backs from the dying
if only for a moment, we see beyond

the wasted remains of the long endured
sickness, we see, at last, the unburdened heart;
this is what it is to love, this is the divine.

Saint-in-the-box
for Helen Cockin

It wasn't chance or good fortune,
my stumbling

was intentional, my obsession
matter of fact

like a bird's
obsession with whistling;

like toothache
or getting up in the morning

to the incessant barking
of dogs.

    *

For six long years this is how I have suffered in the sleep labs, convinced that the pills they give you are designed to keep you from sleep, convinced at last of my duty to foil the madness of the dream professors. Brothers and sisters! Can you blame me for going out of my mind with worry? Every morning the same dogs howling the same regrets…why me? Always me left in the dog house, left to skulk in the coal shed, to gnaw the bones of fossils, lips and tongue, all utterances drunk with dust. Even on the brightest mornings, all dreaming leads back to this.

Once I was close to her!
I was her one true love!

    *

To this purpose alone the screw in the door is turned anti-clockwise, loosening the hinges of loss, allowing us to feel the full benefit of our story-telling, allowing us to believe in the undoing of what's been done. This is the way to invention and this is the world, invention is more than real, it is super-real, it is the air-brush of history gone gaga, the mundane finally transmuted. A tear in the page — neatly does it, a salty trickle to make the ink run, a lie omitting or embellishing whenever it suits.

Once I was close to her!
I was her one true love!

And now my saint, my very own saint, cries diluvial tears, tears big as craters, tears that spill out over the Mare Criseum, wash the dust with sorrow. It is not enough that I have given her all the best lines, all pain and heartache, not enough that I remember her arms and legs and breasts, her singing and her voice so sad from drinking that the song could hardly be sung. It is not enough to remember the words, not enough to remember, not enough.

Once I was close to her!
I was her one true love!

on exile

exiled from your life   i am afraid to leave
the sound of mellifluous rain   accentuating my long sadness

The Last Summer

"Maybe a little love is better than no love at all."
    ANNE SEXTON

You said poetry was your love, your hands, your face…
and I am in need of some of that reassurance
that goes along with your smile as though you were smiling
just for me, I need your reassurance as surely as any son
or lover needs to be needed and loved.
It is May 2006 and I am a man without a woman,
and although this loneliness, this longing to connect
is always with me, it is not so easy to admit to you.
How many admissions can one make
in the lifetime of a single poem?
What confessions come to us in the night, Anne?
What if I were to say, I love you
and when I look at your face, it will always be May 2006
and not that fateful summer of 1974
when you would skinny-dip in the moonlit pool
of those Boston nights beside the wild grass and swamp maples
at 14 Black Oak Road. I was only a boy then
and incapable of adult love, though I loved my own mother
as only a son can. When I say, I love you,
it is not because I have dreamt about you naked
in the cool water, but because I wish to have known you
in the waking world of our every day happenings.
Alas! I will always be a dreamer
and a man who almost drank himself to death
but I will never have known you.
What do men wish for, Anne
beyond the white halter-top summer dress?
What do I wish for in the face and body of a woman?
You are, at once, pensive and mysterious, now laughing
now animated by the sunlight falling on your tanned neck.
I think I will tell you what some men wish for beyond

the white sandals and tanned flesh of heavenly bodies.
We wish to own the past, but not just any past,
and not the past of kings and queens
and not the past of great men and women,
the past of great battles and deeds —
we wish to own the past your other selves belong to.
We wish to wipe out the athletic freshman boys
who filled your dreams for what seems like an eternity
of New England summers, we wish to become
your rock in a storm at sea, your one solitary suitor,
fearless, faithful, forever, your little bit of love.

Acantha

She has taken another lover
to fill the space left untouched
by the men who went before,

she knows not what she seeks
but feels it — real as any other yearning,
buried deep in the human heart.

No man will question her
when she falls asleep at night.
She is unashamed, she longs

for the young man's seed that cracks
the egg, but she will give nothing
of herself except heaven's body

and the accumulation of doubt
of which she is made. Her soul lies
beyond the arcane science

of the star filled sky. Her love
needs no explanation, it is there
and it is not there. It lasts a day

within the century of intense suspicion,
it lasts like rain, if you are lucky,
upon the sand — no more, no more
        than sun can stand.

Season's End

i
move
beneath
you, *Us*, our
over-world, worded bliss,
unending wars, last summer's Death,
(small comfort) the appearance of honeyed youth
conceding the past, loving to touch
hopelessly in-love,
aspiring
to be
as
One

Last Word

It would seem that I'm ill-equipped to deal
with your latest news; how my inadequacies
must disturb you. My room gets lonelier
by the minute and the gloom outside

more oppressive, but I'll not draw back
the blinds, at least, not until my words
can learn how to behave. You'll see then,
my boldness was not misplaced.

Simply to hold you without the narration
of distance, old words and phrases echoing,
my brain wild to the prospects of memory.
I whisper your name. All evening, I pursue

my own reflection, afraid to answer the door,
in case the person standing there isn't you
but some other stranger, not at all convinced,
or even moved by my shadow-play.

*

The other night, do you remember
the other night, my last letter? My language
was so carefree, then. I felt so close to you,
sealing the envelope was almost unthinkable.

You must forgive me for not realising
your other commitments. I'm a fool to hope
for too much. It's just that I can't attend
to anything that happens beyond us.

I found your letter, dated 25th November,
and read with awe the most heartfelt line
you ever wrote me: *Even our frenzied differences*
are compelled to draw us closer than before.

When I read that, I knew we were right
for one another. I'm with you, yet, I'm dumb
before your words, unable to articulate
any response to your honest appraisal of us.

    *

I'm so eager for knowledge of your well-being;
my room's become impos ible without your constant
reassurance. I know this is no good thing
but I'm convinced it can't be any other way.

It seems like forever since you last wrote.
Perhaps you're too ill to write, or worse,
there's someone else and you've forgotten
our little arrangement. I expect the worst.

Afforded these moments to write, separate
and alone, I imagine my life without you,
wondering if my loneliness will affect you,
or will you simply think me overbearing again.

I fear this more than anything. My seriousness
is bound to drive you further away. Just listen to me,
wanting all the time, our failure, willing it,
goading it, yet all along despising and fearing it.

    *

I wonder what's left except what's past.
You must come soon, before my words lose all sense
of proportion. My mood's so dark, if only I could see
the world through your eyes. Then, my dream of us

wouldn't cause this needless distress.
As I moisten the gum on my latest letter,
a sudden light penetrates the black out;
only my thoughts of you keep me from failure.

We're standing by the lake, our lake in the late
afternoon, water laps at our feet. I glance
in your direction, thinking such openness
doesn't deserve mention. The world of bodies

doesn't deserve such light. For an instant,
you're with me, then, the light fades
and I'm back in my little room, with the blinds
drawn and sheets at the window.

    *

How much should I tell you, even now,
though this, in all likelihood
will be the last time I speak your name,
even though it's far too late for excuses.

So many revelations, and not a single one
to make things plain; my love
these lines, possibly our last lines together
are simply signposts to what is unknowable.

I'm painting you because I'm clean out of words.
I've written you and thought for some years
about the possibility of sculpture,
but my hands are clumsy and my words too shy.

Like all the other men who've loved you,
I want you to love me the most.
It's raining and I can see you nude
by the window, and you laugh as though in-love for the first time.

    *

Listening to Satie's Gnossiennes, every note
is struck with you in mind, yet every note
is out of reach and I'm frightened because
I can no longer remember the colour of your eyes

or the shape of your fingers stretching
to make the keys. The realm of pure emotions,
the world without conditions is closing
and the realisation is unbearable because it is impassable.

My hand flounders across the page,
incapable of writing anything reasonable.
I'm unable to quantify how I feel in any normal sense
of the word. It's no longer sufficient to say:

I want you. I need you. I love you.
My words have become fractious, they bray
at the door, imploring you to let them in,
only their noisy insistence falls away like dreams.

An Agnostic's Prayer

When I tell you that I love your Audrey Santo:
the girl, whom, it is said, performs miracles
in her sleep, it is because I know her in my heart
as though she were my own flesh and blood,

when I knelt beside her bed in the late morning
all the world stood still, all my previous life
came to me as if in slow motion, acted out
behind the retina as though I had been given

the gift of my own memory for the first time;
I was not disturbed nor did I regret the course
my life had taken, I wished nothing then
for myself in that lonely room, but I could not help

feeling sorrow for the girl with the unfathomable
dreams, so I said to her, 'I will pray for you, my Audrey Santo,'
and she said back to me in a voice gentle as prayer,
'what can I do for you my brother in destiny?'

And I was not astounded nor did I find myself
disbelieving the sound of the voice inside my head,
I only wished to take the darkness she had known
these past nineteen years – away from her eyes

so she could see the world as I saw it, but then
it came to me more clearly than the winter sun,
perhaps Audrey Santo was blessed in ways
I could never comprehend, perhaps she really was

the waking world's connection with God.

Minotaur's Woe

Nothing escapes my attention. Here in the maze
I am king of all the world's confusions,
      blind alley ways,
and the afflicted leading the afflicted.

It's quite simple, there are only ever unhappy endings;
in the dark, we are all love sick or sick of love
where the walls tower above us like walls
towering above us like walls towering like walls,
and back among the back streets I tear my heart
out to my heart's content.
                        Who will come forward
to steal my crown? The boy wonder will not fight
me now. Inside the tangle of the head
I do not think of ease or grace, but worry instead
about my loss, my swollen appetite.

Canal Poem

i met a stranger today   a bit lonely   a bit sad
he took a poem from the breast pocket of his jacket

and threw it into the dead canal   where it sank
with bicycles   pumps   clips   chemicals   all manner

of wreckage   afterwards   he said he felt lighter somehow
more able to cope with the random business of sorrow

his tears started   treacherous with the rain
the canal stretched and stretched into the next lock

Lost Souls

I heard of a man who dreamt whole operas
for you when he slept, but they could never be scored
and so you could never hear them. I heard
of a boy who waited all night for you outside
your window in the snow, until his breath froze still.
I heard of choirs that had stopped their singing,
and divinities that had outlived their usefulness.
This is how it is with memory, the world freezes
over, the late frost hardens unfamiliar ground,
longings flare up, and in the dawn a boy is ruined –
this is the only music for a while, we conjure
these apparitions together in our going away
from each other, we are left with only tricks
the mind can play to assuage a heart in turmoil.

Solace

I see your dreams in the night mists
bound around my solitude
like an unwanted guest on the turret steps.

Like so much else, the language spoken is secret,
the stolen caresses more resolute
than what time would usually allow.

There are no reasons for this trickery
only that which is left by starlight
on those nights when the moon is barely seen.

On this stage the dream will be made real
by the cravings for freedom
and for the dissatisfied mind – freedom

will be satisfied in some temporary place –
remembering nothing before,
this passion will not outlast the daylight.

River of Blood

"I end as a traitor to my party, a traitor who must be shot."
SERGEI MRACHKOVSKY, *22 August, 1936*

Night in Coyoacan. The darkness heavy with fear and longing.
Natalia Sedova awakens from her dreams. Gunshots
ring out in the Mexican dark... "They are shooting here,
in our room," cries Natalia, her voice, shrill and frightened.

The Old Man moves slowly at first. He is not afraid to die
and cares little for his own safety – he fires after his attackers
with his revolver, but it is no use, Siqueiros and his men
disappear into the May dawn and a pall of silence descends.

Quietly then, he remembers the names: Zinoviev, Kamenev,
Sokolnikov, Bubnov, Bukharin, Serebrayakov, Smilga,
Berzin, Krestinsky, Antonov-Ovseyenko, Joffe, Kiselev,
Preobrazhensky and Varvara Nikolayevna Yakovleva.

Lev Davidovich knows there will be no reunion of old Bolsheviks,
the Old Guard are gone into dust, they have been forcibly removed
from the scene of history and they will speak no more in the rabid air,
they have given their last brave breaths but the end was inevitable.

Trotsky recalls his trips into the mountains to collect cactuses,
and Natasha milling the grain for baking bread and tortillas.
He pulls his grandson, Sieva closer to his chest and calls out
to his wife, "Natasha, they have let us live for one more day!"

Farewell, Leon Lvovich

*"Together with our boy has died everything
that still remained young within us."*
    LEON TROTSKY

What terrible suspicions come to us in the dark? Sedov
is no more, the Moscow executioners have struck again,
they have expunged Leon Lvovich without a shot being fired.

No more will he ride the Moscow street cars of his youth.
No more will he clean the snow from the Moscow streets.
No more will he step out under the Parisian sky with his beloved
        wife, Jeanne.

He has gone to join his brother, Sergei and his sisters, Zinaida
and Nina Lvovna in death, only now will he gain the peace
he was denied in life by the ghouls of the Thermidor.*

For three days his mother and father mourn in the darkness
of their private room and they are changed irrevocably.
Now only the vengeance of history can console the Old Man.

Not until Stalin has been consigned to that chamber of horrors
reserved for the Neros and Caligulas will Trotsky
ever breathe easily again. His younger self is gone forever.

What dreams may still abound lie in the victory of the Fourth
International. *Our only weapon is the truth... The truth will emerge...*
Sedov's words are etched into our minds until the end of time.

---

* Thermidor is that moment in the development of a revolution when the masses begin to withdraw from active intervention in history and the original leadership of the revolution is replaced by a conservative bureaucracy.

For A Fistful Of Earth

I took a fistful of earth from the gardens
where you were living, I carried it with me
for days and then weeks, I didn't understand why
at first I carried it to and fro about town –
I only knew I didn't want to let it go,

and in the soil I saw something solid
and magical that I could hold on to like a comforter
or a charm, it didn't matter that it hurt me
to clench it in my fist. No one remarked
'how strange' it was, or 'how inappropriate'.

Passers by accepted it as though it was my destiny –
this is what I had lived for, loved for.
No one thought I was mad or even mildly foolish
and yet it was almost certainly the case –
a handful of earth couldn't make up for what was lost.

It couldn't save the curlew from the fox,
bring out the thrushes from the trees,
or make their little voices sing just for me.
It couldn't ease the places where your hands should be,
or bring back heaven to the living man…

> I need a fistful of earth to fill the spaces
> where our bodies have been –
> I need my body to be with your body.

Calypso

You have retreated into the console
of another man, yet what you seek
lies beyond the reach of mortal flesh.

When the sun falls below the western
horizon, you will go to him as though
he were your only lover, and he, in his turn

will give himself to you without question,
as though you were the only woman
he has ever known, and the old lies

will be told during and after your bodies
have worn out the promises of love
even the young have long lost faith in.

From one lost soul to another will pass
the long history of earthly disappointments
and you know the moon will not sing

for you, or light your way quite as it did
before. In the waste of broken promises
you lie awake at night unable to dream

and the soul is lost to the deceit of the flesh.
What is left behind is as lost to heaven
as the furthest reaches of the abyssal plain.

Swamp Meeting

Years later we meet in a house
where neither feel sure of conversation
      that can only drift
      backwards.

At first there is reluctance, we eye
the other's seriousness like birds
      in the snow, fratching
      over scraps.

Not so much absorbed in each other
as in ourselves, we argue. Too much
      and then, too little
      has changed.

Only the accusations of cruelty remain
the same. The tall trees are motionless
      in the dark, the waters
      of the garden quiet,

but the thrushes' fear of undercurrents
names this place. Marsh. Mire. Bog.
      We are certain only of this:
      after the pubs have closed

and the last train's been missed,
what's changed seems less important.
      Other involvements pale.
      The light fades.

In the morning, you talk of periods and trains,
of where you must be and where you must go.
      Even now, I need to know
      whether you'll look back

before the corner finally obscures you
from view, as I watch you hurrying away
      through the mud, hurrying
      through the dark mud.

Fall from Grace

Be gone, jealous heart, hush now
while the sun infects this quiet cavity
between bedroom and bathroom,
where both lovers are still standing.

What did we expect from two bodies,
but the desire to unravel the inscrutable,
the sensual anonymous self
locked in the others mortal flesh?

Was it anything more than daydream,
to think it meant anything at all,
beyond the physical act of consolation,
in a world pressing for meaning?

From the senseless to the sensible,
while the secrets burn in the soft tissue
and lies are told to all that we care for;
we move towards our own human ends

creating these catastrophes, as we pass,
from place to place and time to time.
These liaisons that surely define us,
tear down all that we would ask of love.

Ageing Sisyphus

Sometimes he will shout out in his sleep,
'Friends! Lovers! Lover!' of which he has none,
'leave the lights on across town –
from lofty drawing room to lofty bed-sit,
that we might share our private hurts.'
And if by some miracle, his old eyes
were ever to see beyond the oval
of hills that stale the dreamer's horizons,
we might even concede it for ourselves,
that the hero of this piece, was indeed
an expert, not only in torment
but in the exigencies of solitude
and not as many would have us believe,
nothing more than a sot with a sore head.

Autumn Leaving

1.

You left me in the dark
kicking through mounds
of dead leaves in the wetness.

2.

I rushed home
raincoat fastened against
the Dostoyevskian landscape.

Mica

For you, I will be everything
a poet should be and feed the dispossessed
outside of every holy shrine.

For you, I will sell love-poems to the Jesuits
and they will take sustenance
from them as though it were the new blood of Christ.

For you, I will ride into the lions den
and face every enemy
to free the poor man and the slave.

For you, I will denounce the evil doings
of the despots armies
and march to meet them at dawn.

For you, I will save the heron from the fox
and pen happy endings
for all the broken and the lame.

For you, I will re-write the book of pain
and bring laughter
into the wards of disease and disaster.

For you, I will marry solitude
(for I know solitude) and keep my inner quiet
to myself.

Autumn Rises

As all is temporary, my love, so in this bed you lie
and though we are far from strangers, we are lost
for any gestures that would comfort the other.

We have exhausted all the possibilities within us
for this or that particular future, but the game goes on
with unequal billing, and one of us must always lose.

It is this way because the hanging raindrops
would not soak the ground where we would remember
the spell to right the path. We have gone beyond

the charms of mist and light that bear resemblance
to our former passing, when we were as children
under the watchful eye of the morning cherry blossom.

Nothing could keep us together, not even for a day,
but when I think of my body next to yours,
I want to pass through the arches of your thighs, forever.

The Unanswered Question

i.m. Bill Lawson

In the inky belly of nights like these
when the moon lies

within a hair's breadth of touching,
a single cloud

will carry with it all the sorrows
of memory;

all but stationary,
imperceptible, except for starlight

striking its outer edges,
we will measure

its doubtful progress towards
the sensible horizon

and with sudden recourse to regret:
speaking

termless rhymes,
we will throw the doors wide

to our shred of sky, patch
the hours with fragments of light and air.

Transformation

What is left when mouth no longer touches mouth
but the dumb recollection of kissing,
the implacable dream of sensuous longing?

Whatever it was to know such kindness
passes from the account of the self, as though
it was less than real, less than wholly human.

In less than a second, everything changes
and there is no more communion of the flesh.
Our hearts will not meet in some future place.

Nor will I marvel at your matchless thighs
or touch once more, your flawless skin –
the unblemished world I had become so fond of.

But at least for you and I, there is no treachery
involved in moving on, we elope
to disparate shores with only rapture in mind.

Although we now inhabit unfamiliar moons,
we will remember what has passed from sight
and each time we summon up the memory,

it will change us over and over again;
in this way can we be renewed,
in this way can we begin to live over.

In A Rage With Allen Ginsberg

Found once again shamelessly in bed with you, where I'm madder than you are, infinitely so, and I've been clear of the funny farm a full three years. I'm with you in a rage, experiencing the truth in all its mad glory, and the enemy is still nowhere to be seen. I'm with you in a rage, and I still can't quite believe it – of all the crazy thinking, of all the screwed up goings on – all the wild eyed schemes. I'm with you in a rage, and my father is still lecturing me on the merits of reading poetry and committing it to memory. I'm with you in a rage while the televisions ring out in the public bars and shopping malls with the divine message: 'the West is the best.'

I'm with you in a rage, and somewhere across the globe, incendiary bombs are being dropped on the homes of the unsuspecting poor. I'm with you in a rage where the doubts of centuries are blossoming in our hearts like some new sickness. I'm with you in a rage – two giant insomniacs, no more sleepy for our acquaintance – while the progress of the 21st century tramples our children underfoot. I'm with you in a rage with the poems and songs of our brothers burned into our minds, etched onto our tongues like some new language. I'm with you in a rage, and although we are not John Lennon and Yoko Ono, our message is no less momentous, no less relevant, no less heartfelt.

Will our comrades ever forgive us for thinking poetry could make a difference? Fellow poets, the historical moment is upon us, we must rush the stage of history with our chap books and our manifestos. Forget your private hurts, I love you all in my own way. I loved the girls in the asylum too, though our kisses are gone forever. Ah, toilers of the page and soil, we will never submit to those who would enslave us. We know the greatest terror resides at home, the terror is what sedates us and what keeps us in chains. A hundred years passes, and the only difference is that exploitation isn't meant to feel like exploitation any more.

O democracy with your promise that we can all share in the spoils – we reject the white picket fence and the church jamboree. O poets! O philosophers! O downtrodden masses! We are here to claim what is ours...

The Last Stand of Salvador Allende

"*¡Viva Chile! ¡Viva el pueblo! ¡Vivan los trabajadores!*"
SALVADORE ALLENDE

They say that before you die, your entire life flashes
before your eyes. They say it plays itself out like a movie
before the curtains finally close on the conscious mind.

Outside La Moneda, the *coup d'etat* gathers its forces,
inside, the President's supporters are bewildered and isolated,
only the President knows what the end demands of him.

He knows the General's coup will turn back the clock
of history. But he knows he will not take exile or resign.
He will not give one inch to the men who would deny him,

the men of violence who would drown Chile in blood.
First, the past, then, the future is played out
in his mind's eye – where he imagines himself dead.

Salvador Allende addresses the people of Chile on the radio:
History is ours… Tomorrow will belong to the people…
Long live Chile! Long live the people! Long live the workers!

He has nothing left in the world to give now but his own life.
This will be his last act of defiance – we are what we do.
He puts his rifle to his head and pulls the trigger on a brave life.

Lonely Fighter

While you were dreaming with another
in the next room,
I wrote you letters, soliloquy's, discourses on love,
All night I stared at the written pages
knowing I would never send them,
knowing I would never change your mind.

No matter how many times I wrote: 'I miss you',
I knew my heart was a lonely fighter in this,
as in all else, I wished for your embrace,
but the embrace given yesterday
is quickly forgotten today.
Now I am a man in need of someone's hand.

This morning I took a razor blade and scored 'I LOVE'
into the underside of my forearm.
I did it, most of all, for you –
although you will never see it,
although it means little or nothing in reality,
although losing you is not the end for me entirely.

You have left me alone in the bleak mid-winter
with cuts deeper than any I could make,
but I will not die today because of it, or even within the year.
The end can last a day or an eternity
and I will love again
but nothing will ever be the same, never the same.

William S. Burroughs Dead

The old man has taken all manner of personal effects with him –
like Pharaoh he will not lie dead for long in his green velvet
Moroccan vest and his grey fedora. Soon he will step out
clutching his favourite hickory cane with its rosewood finish

and scare the birds in Central Park. Soon the gold brocade trim
on that Moroccan vest will be worth a million dollars. Already,
I can hear him say, 'I feel like a million dollars,' then he will add,
'I feel lousy,' and we won't miss the sense of irony in his voice.

But he will step out down Broadway brandishing his snub-nose
special and shoot at the moon just for luck before giving
thanks for the Daisy Cutter, the Popeye missile and depleted
uranium. Yes folks, he will give thanks where thanks is due,

we can be sure of that. Thanks for the tireless war on terror,
thanks for the blood, thanks for the all American dreamers,
thanks for the mighty, the willing, the brave, thanks
for the hawks – those hard beaked purveyors of all that's sane

and good and true. Thanks one and all. The penny spins
and nothing remains the same. Mistah Burroughs – he alive
and he is having none of it. The new millennium is reason
enough to destroy the old gods. He is a man on a mission.

And he will not betray us, or lie to us, or tell us tall tales
or fairy tales or skimp on the truth – not even for our own good.
No Sirree! He will tap dance his way into the living rooms
of the poor, the downtrodden, the perplexed, the anonymous

multitudes and sing with all his passion about the unnatural
order of things in the breathing, feeling world where children
kneel before the cross and the dark barbarian hordes
are always, ineluctably, just one step away from the truth.

Oh we know William of old – he will not let us down,
he will not dip out at the last minute with a bad case
of the jitters. He will not be enticed into the gilded palaces
of deception, give way to the arbiters of reason, reality

or reaction, make out with the denizens of clean living,
give in to the houses of the holy, or give death a second chance.
And we will welcome the old man as we would any other brother
        or sinner –
only then will it be said, we are breaking the walls of our prison.

Seems So Long Ago

I do not know how many times I drew you naked
in those last weeks before all our songs
out-played themselves on the stereo:

how many nights I called your name
from knocked out telephone boxes
and wrecked sash windows overlooking the park.

Although I have not given-in entirely to memory,
I feel undone – like a man wanting
too much from the comfort of our embrace.

When I am alone, like tonight, I remember
our touching on the kitchen floor
among the garbage and the dirty laundry,

I imagine drawing you then, as you go down
for your goal, savouring the magic
of which each is made.

We would move heaven and earth to go back
but that old road would not suffice
and we would not have it for more than just a day.

We are not mountains; only children dreaming
of yesterday. Only in dreams will we brave
the curious rain and roar of our desires.

Requiem For A Kiss

We loiter in the old shop doorway
and behind the factory wall where we grow
phantom-like in the half-dark
that does engulf the beating heart.

Unaccustomed to the gaiety and noise –
the hoof and cart of our own past,
we come together in this foreign land,
this foreign century to stand our ground.

We speak after so many years of silence,
so many years of quiet surrender
to the stars, the ragged boot and the gnarled hand
that would grab at the grubby pavements

of our forgotten dreams, it is unlikely
that any of it could make a difference.
It has become impossible to regain
what is lost in the endless, featureless nights.

Two lovers embrace, kiss, fall away
and even this moment is stolen
from the stomach-turning ground that would deny
even this most human of happenings.

Versts

for Marina Tsvetayeva

We must eat our fill when we can,
though the stomach shrinks with grief and hunger.
We must assert ourselves bodily,
though not a soul would listen to our sad pronouncements.

We know how many journeys end in tears,
but we know our feet must tread the weary path.
We know the age of lust must have its monsters,
but we know our woe cannot last forever.

When I am dead, my heart adrift on its last journey,
I will be as powerless to take shelter with you
as any other man seeking comfort in your caresses,
and though we would await the new century

in our lonely rooms, we would not wish
to leave pity as our only embrace.
Time carries all our secrets to the grave,
and love, in its own way, takes care of the dead.

Marinka, we will meet somewhere in time,
and half the world will smile like me and you.
We will not sleep then, until the dawn sun,
like gentle rain, assuages all our fears.

I lift my skinny fists like antennas to heaven.
I look in your pure direction.
I kiss you once again, for old time's sake.
I am a man who does not wish to die.

Tonight

My dream is you, but my seriousness
will not last. Only this is true. When the door
finally closes on this brutality, and the hand

that reaches, only reaches out for sorrow
you will muse for a while on what we
so readily allow, discard, as though, having

forgotten how to touch, love or even want
the other, reasons for being together
have given way to reasons for being apart.

But tonight these things will not be
spoken. Joy. Celebration. Love. Only darkness
coming, with fistfuls of uncertainty.

In His Time Of Dying

Penniless as always and now intoxicated, his body a dull ache in someone else's headache, drunk with pain and worry and regret, drunk with love and even drunk with lust, the injured man considered his position. The oval of faces that loomed above him looked ugly and remote like unwanted guests at a birthday party. Clumsily, they pressed forward into an ever tighter ball that blotted out the sky.

'All that humanity,' he thought, 'and yet no cement for the human bond.'

Curious at the sight of the crooked man, they crowded closer to pinpoint the spot. Unable to move he imagined himself a latter day saint or saviour among men. No one would deny him that now. He wondered what was certain. Was it certain that his wife had left only two nights before, or was he the one who'd been asked to leave and in a blind rage done the leaving? The semantics weighed on his mind.

'To depart. To disappear. To quit.'

So much tautology. He couldn't make up his mind. Was it certain that he was bleeding, or even injured at all, or was it just the sensation of rain soaking his clothes?

'At last,' he thought, 'this is the recognition I deserve.'

How purposeful it all seemed, as if that moment in the rain was meant to happen, the whole wretched world watched and cared what happened to him now. And with that he closed his eyes and lost consciousness.

An Ending

And then it happens, another star in the light universe goes out
and the star gazers are baffled by its demise –
thinking as they did that it was such an immature star.

From nothing, through nothing, to nothing (says the philosopher) –
we are alone here, this much we know, without seeing
the quickening that would leave the night sky dark forever.

And then it happens, in that not too distant place
where linear time is measured in moments not aeons –
the heart closes to the possibility of connection.

And the thoughts of lovers were yet to declare
an interest in creation beyond the reach of the naked eye,
give birth to the incessant beating of their own ending.

Willow Lane

- *Old woman, why are you crying on such a fine summer's evening?*

- *Haven't you heard, my son?*

- *I have heard little tonight, except the hum of rush hour traffic.*

- *A terrible tragedy has occurred.*

- *But everything looks so ordinary. The street resembles any other.*

- *Haven't you noticed the willow trees — how they are weeping?*

- *But willow trees will always weep. That is why they are so named.*

- *Haven't you seen the sky, my son?*

- *The sky looks like any other July sky.*

- *Oh, no, no, no. The sky has fallen in on itself. And now there is an emptiness that can't be filled. They are gone, never to return to the living earth.*

Nie przejmuj się [1]

What on earth is he thinking,
the guard
in the Gauntanamo tower?

Clearly, he is not reading Noam Chomsky,
so often he falls asleep with his cap over his eyes
he does not know we are watching him,
nor that all around
the songs of the inmates are carried by the wind,

nor further, that comrade Chomsky
duly marks the solemnity of this occasion
in one of his many notebooks,
before the emeritus professor dresses for dinner
ahead of the President Elects inauguration.

---

[1] Polish for don't worry

Diogenes Checkmates

It has been suggested by chess enthusiasts
that the game is a microcosm of world events,
(white pawn to king's knight four) that
stalemate is a metaphor for the east/west
debacle (black pawn to queen four).
However, some thinkers have suggested
that the game is rather wooden, like bad tragedy
or a king's ransom, (white pawn to king's bishop
three) raising the point, who's fooling who,
if all are equally baffled? (black queen
to rook five – fool's mate).

The Zoo

In the dead of the day, the eyes came
to act as witnesses at the physician's door,

errands were run by the strongest twins
to the crematorium. Inside the wire

their eyes shone like amber, coral and pearl,
bloodied eyes, half-blind and strangely vacant

peered into the office of the man they knew
as 'uncle'. On the far wall, mutilated eyes

were pinned to boards like butterflies wings
in a collectors display. These were the eyes

of Francesca, Potyo, Tibi and Georges,
Mikos, Ada, Masha and Sara. Faceless now,

without sentiment or reason, the eyes stare
into the pitiless room as history unfolds

before scalpel and needle. Faithless, lost,
bewildered, the children of the fire

wait their turn. Soon they too will burn,
soon enough their eyes will be also garnered.

Memorial

Half the world away, two sisters lie dead —
their young bodies burned
beyond all earthly recognition, victims of a map.
They bore no malice, knew of no sins,
nor of the ungodly will
to unleash a shoah against their people.
In their all too brief lives
they lived with the burden of oppression,
playing girlish games in the courtyard of their father.

Half the world away, the Asliyeh sisters,
Samah, 13, and Salwa, 18, lie dead
in the bombed Tel al-Zaatar neighbourhood
of the Beirut refugee camp.
Let us remember their good natured play
now all generosity and solace is gone —
for all who would hear us
we offer a prayer, Samah and Salwa
lest we forget, lest we forget.

Why I Am Not A Sculptor

Like the poet, Frank O'Hara, I am not a sculptor,
but a poet (at least) according to my friends,
I am a man who passes himself off as a poet.
Why? Because poetry is the property of no one.
Because stone and point would not obey
the commands of a man obsessed with oblivion.
Because the light universe is no place
for a man who lives in dreams.
Because I am in awe of Igor Mitoraj.

I am alone in the too darkened quarries
of my imagination, picking through the debris of time,
exhuming the dead, picking through the bones
of my poor dead relatives. What am I to do
without hammer or chisel? I am too many centuries old
to start over. And I am dumb beside you
because we can no longer talk or laugh at the silliness
of being who we are. More centuries pass.

Because I am not a sculptor, I am forced
      on to the back foot once again.
Because I am not a sculptor, I am transfixed
by a life rendered in stone. And I say to the sculptor,
'I cannot suppress my desire to be a sculptor.'
And the sculptor answers back, 'I cannot suppress
my desire to be a poet.' And perhaps we are, each of us,
what the other wishes to be, if only
for a short time – in the margins of some other story.

Photo: Christopher Zaleski

MARK A. MURPHY was born in 1969 in the UK where he still lives. He studied philosophy (BA) at Stafford and poetry (MA) at Huddersfield University. His poems have been published in over 100 magazines and ezines world wide, including *Poetry New Zealand*, *Poetry Scotland*, *The Warwick Review* (UK), *Istanbul Literature Review* (Turkey), *The Paris Atlantic Journal* (France), *The American Dissident* (US), *The Tampa Review* (US), *Left Curve* (US) and *The Stinging Fly* (Ireland). He is the creator and editor of the online poetry journal *POETiCA*. This is his debut collection.